LONGSHIP

JESSICA MAYHEW

LONGSHIP

WINNER OF THE MELITA HUME
POETRY PRIZE 2018

First published in 2019
by Eyewear Publishing Ltd
Suite 333, 19-21 Crawford Street
Marylebone, London W1H 1PJ
United Kingdom

Cover design and typeset by Edwin Smet
Printed in England by TJ International Ltd, Padstow, Cornwall

The right of Jessica Mayhew to be identified as author of
this work has been asserted in accordance with section 77
of the Copyright, Designs and Patents Act 1988
ISBN 978-1-912477-89-0

Dedicated with love to AH

Jessica Mayhew's first pamphlet,
Someone Else's Photograph, was published by Crystal Clear
Creators in 2012. After graduating from UCL with a Masters
in English Literature, she spent a year working in south-east
Asia, and during this time wrote a pamphlet, *Amok*, which was
published by Eyewear in 2015. Her poetry, fiction and essays
have been published in magazines including *Ambit, Stand, Staple,
Brittle Star, Magma*, and *The Interdisciplinary Literary Studies
Journal*. She has also given readings at the Nottingham
and Ledbury Poetry Festivals. Jessica currently lives in
Hertfordshire with her street dog, Bracken.

TABLE OF CONTENTS

THE  MELITA HUME
POETRY PRIZE

Jessica Mayhew is the 2018 winner of the
Melita Hume Poetry Prize. She received £2,000 and this
publication. The 2018 Judge was Colette Sensier,
whose comments read:

I was lucky enough to discover many bright new voices on
the Melita Hume shortlist but *Longship* was notable for its
creation of what feels like a living, interconnected world.
The manuscript blurs myth and modern life, moving
between ventriloquism of the gods of the Norse myths, and
the griefs of present-day bereavement, love and – portrayed
in fabulous language on the brink between surrealist
metaphor and natural wonder - climate apocalypse. I felt
I was in the presence of a strong and determined voice,
as Mayhew's powerful control of language called back to
Norse forms with firm alliterative lines and bold images.
Many poems feel like communications between our modern
selves and deeper, older impulses and ways of living in
nature – ways which in Mayhew's hands feel accessible
and shockingly real. I look forward to seeing *Longship*, and
hopefully many other Mayhew volumes, in print.

LONGSHIP

Snow is the letter slid under the door
that makes everything strange.

Wind, wild from the long howl south,
strips the streets. Crows wink from murals

at houses, boasting in primary colours
at beyond: moss-rock, water smoke, pigeon glass.

We shivered in our coats,
summoned to the church and later, shroudside,
a longship carved onto her stone.

GULLVEIG

Cheek to the cold stone floor
and they might tell you that
you're not like other women,

they like a challenge.
A bitch trembles in the corner
with her tail down.

Husbands find wives' dresses
torn and bloodied in the morning,
soles threaded with thorns,
strange roots drying in the sun.

Outside, wolves shout,
sky hagged with their calling.

Pierced through at their feet, I tell them,
everyone can be free once,
the same way that every mushroom
can be eaten once. I have the words
to thank the very blood
soaking the kindling,
three times burnt, thrice reborn.

THE MAGPIE'S LOCKET

All the coats we had, and handed down
from eldest to youngest,
took off like a skein of crows

once the rings came off, stayed off.
The beech sundered the house straight through

spilled sunlight as gold ink across the three of us,
everything dead or gone to ground
to rouse in some distant Spring
when we might say: *Here.*
This is the house we used to live in.

We disturbed the black and white birds,
purring over silver.

As if in a dream
you blew on the tips of your fingers
to feel for their eggs,
and risked abandonment
from the mother, the father.

Wordless, then, it was not me
who found the locket hanging
in the magpie's nest of our hair,
unravelled jumpers, purloined tinsel
in colours going back years,
but when I opened it, gods help me,
my own face was inside.

HOW TO WALK ON ICE

Trudging back from the *Queen's Head*,
we stopped to watch a coal-furled coot
pitch itself across the ice. We furrowed
down the hill, snow frosting our cuffs,
fingers buckled in each other's sleeves.
'There,' you traced the unpacked sky,
the stars, through a shawl of cider-breath
and smoker's-terrace cigarettes,
'the *Plough, Big Dipper,* the *String-Of-Pearls.*'
Stamping through grit-salt
under Christmas bulbs shivering on brick,
I thought how the snow beading your hair
and these scattered constellations
looked nothing like pearls.

FERNS

When the fern unfurls, slowly,
with the anatomy of keys

ignore the chamber of ivy,
the plate-locked lichen.

Coy fingers unlatch hidden things
and the will to find them,

pointing through pale bars of birch,
the bloom of mushrooms on wet wood,

to the girl they pulled down
from the very highest branches,

her bare feet mossed with bark-rub,
hair already fronded with frost.

YGGDRASIL

Ants freckled the bark,
the tree knotted and bunched,
mist-rimed like sweat on the skin
of a horse, nine nights ridden.

Bridled, I hung boughwards,
blossom-bright in moonshine,
or else blind, meaded sun-yellow,
Autumn, and all the shades of trauma —

I speared myself. Slowed the blood's
constant gallop. Watched as the garnets
shook themselves free of the root,
the old iron claim of the heart,
grown ferrous. Dusk rusted the leaves.

VǪLVA

That one far-off star plucked, repeating in fire,
before I even realise that my eyes are open –
Odin, I know that it is you, feathered in the dark.
The things I speak are in the ground,
my tongue earthed, teeth seeded, roots
staked through my ribs, one by one.
The early frost shocks the gourd
that was my heart. I still know the pulse,
your three honeyed days of wakefulness – thief!
You gave her your word, and you should be ashamed.
How could I even tell you, describe
the violence of water, from rain to snow,
the seeking stream, and fetters of ice?
Yes, Baldr and Nana shall feast before the thaw.
Do not ask me again. Let me go.

BALDR

Dusty quartz and ore
bolted through with gold,

raw wood, oak and apple, sap-wet,
speared, all swore me no mar.

I'd kiss flames from flint,
dredge water for dousing

from the hooves of the waves
and the ships that saddled them.

I let the bear nuzzle my neck,
mouth foaming and fanged –

bolder, I leapt from cliffs, woundless.
I winged up the high pines,

swung from rookeries.
From there, I could watch in secret

my blind brother, face turned
to the sunset, feeling the night

come on like a bruise, a gentle harm.

FRIGG

Like quaking aspen
my hands rooted together

every time I asked

eelgrass, egret, tufted lynx,
reindeer smoking breath.

Hare flexed, one eye bold, heart thundering.
Fox, jaws slick with yolk, sympathised;
she was a mother too.

Soon my knees knew the ground again,
pressing beggingullies in the wet grass.
Daisies soothed the bruises,
and poppies languished, nodding.

When I climbed the rocks,
each stumble was the shock
of knowing what was coming.
Nettles nipped my ankles.

Oath it – if not for my boy, then –

when I spoke, my tongue split through,
and I tasted the blood of what I was asking,
the mistletoe trembling, too small to swear.

WHEN THEY ASK WHAT I TOLD YOU

Like a black bird, turning into the wind,
now too far above to see, your last heartbeat
lapped softly. The words I taught you
finally useless: hawthorn, halfmoon.

Sunspilled in the fenland, everything blazed.
I will make myself forget the horse blood,
putting my lips to your cold ear,

those three sharp notes I sung to myself
over and over, trying to lure the sap
from the cut branches, coax the flowers,
your cloaked eyes, open again.

HELROAD

Birds on the plains, white and grey against the blue fields,
it must have rained once, the air still smells of it,
and the earth pocked with so many footprints
through the weeping cowslip, wintergreen and hemlock,
a bitter garland, fire dripping from my kindling.

Could I bear to stay here, stay quiet, living,

living, which is to say, learning to lose things,
beginning with the skin from your knees, virginity.
Each time you hear a bird sing, the song before flits,
lovers, parents, you cannot cling any more than you could
grasp smoke, a fistful of water. Even your own face
falls deeper each day into a mirror you cannot clear
even by holding your breath, wiping with a sleeve.

But in the end, I would forget too.
After all, who could imagine marching into the dark,
and demanding, just demanding the one you loved, back.

LUNULA

Bones, and less than bones
are the hands that held this last,
bronze pendant worn thin, horns to the earth.

In the car park, a boy is smoking a cigarette.
Imagine, now, you are pulling down the moon.

Heave one hand over the other,
rope or chain, it doesn't matter

sink to your knees   it will get brighter
you squint   the stars are unconcerned

craters wax clearer.

He has dropped his cigarette,
exhales smoke like a hex   what have you done

Just pull harder. In long noon shadow,
dust sifts your faces grey.

A car alarm warbles. First one, then many,

your hair lifts, raindrops strain towards it

what have you done   what have you done.

in the distance   the ocean bucks   you can smell it.

THE KNACK

From above, a midnight cyclist
swan-glides along tarmac rivers.

The cleaner yawns, office neon
flicking off behind him. Outside,

the last of the leaves are silted
below the trees. She could swoop

and touch the very highest tips,
now she has the knack, unpuzzling

streets from hedgerows,
fields fallen open to moonlight,

deer tuning one ear to her leaving,
herd rippling. Dew blossoms on her lashes.

In the low cloud, she can taste salt,
a sea lane in the dark, peppered with stars,

and when he stirs beside her in his sleep
she presses her lips to the back of his neck,

the curtains winging from the open window,
remembering the right way of falling.

BACK WHEN WE WERE BEARS

Lured through a riot of snowberry and red-splurge,
rosy with cheap wine, leaves all lit up yellow with sunset.
                              Sequinned dresses slithered to the ground
                              flashing like hunted salmon.

Pollen-slick, we found our rumoured fangs
amongst the brunt of bark and bodies.
Daisy-petalled love-me-nots down our necks,
                              our bare throats,
              we left as a trail to find our way back.

The ruptured calyx of our pelts
snagged in pines, stiff with sap,
shadows pinned with their needles.

              Sometimes, night uncovers
pastel bedrooms, soothed by cream cottons and silks,
cloud savaging the setting constellations, *Ursa Minor.*
Somewhere, those furs might still be hanging
like washing, shrunken, child-size.

SEA LANES

Before she left, we found the ocean
in strange places.

Her teeth pearled in the glass
by the window,

she used to laugh, say that we rolled
our vowels all around our mouth,
before we spat them out.

We never learned her own clipped tongue,
or the taste for salt on porridge,
brine seeking vein, a way back home.

All night, we watched the herring
swim overhead in great flashes,

a slick aurora above the town.
The next day, the lawns were littered,

before the knife shone against the
scales, throat opened, belly split,

the cooper's boot, the oar's labour, the shock of sky,

the gullet-slide beneath the floodtides.

SIX DAY WAR

Under your gaze,
I dip fingertips in water
to roll rice, vine leaves,

as you did in Egypt,
before you fled,
your tomatoes misting
in the silent kitchen
until they oozed, collapsed.

Newspaper gaped voicelessly, spelling ruin
over holes in the floors, doors, ceilings,
even the air was cracked –

At the border, your mother in tears,
forced to hand over the case
holding the locks of your dead brother's hair –

but now, each palm-cupped rice roll,
is a charm against getting lost,
each leaf is a prayer against having to chose
what you can leave behind, what you can live without.

THE BRINK

Each day, the water is a little higher.
The wooded walkways for fisherman
worn down, speckled with bent nails.

I'd walk the way I walked as a teenager,
for hours, the skyline exhaustingly same,
fields open and heavy with grey cows,

heads all bowed, bald as bone
in the starlight. The moon too
has edged through the warren of trees.

When you were at the brink,
I'd stop at the very foamridge of water,
the little lap lap lap at the cuffs

of my trousers, like a child tugging
at my sleeve, *look look*.
Wondered if what cradled you
would keep you, pull you down.

AFTER THE SIESTA

Lemons smoulder
sticky and deflated on the glazed tiles
under the slow creep of ants,
now that she is not here to pick them.

All day we have cut and hauled,
dismantling the orchard
from the uncountry of desert.
Here, even your gaze will wither.

Prickly with lemon bark, we lie,
sun-shocked and sucking splinters,
knowing that below, the thorns
she never seeded are already stirring.

FIRST WINTER

You say you didn't think the sky could hold so much.
This place welters in snow-light,
footfalls creak on stairs, then carpet.

Outside, fir branches wag under weight,
under the whirred ricochet of wing-beats.
The last of the leaves hang, damp like socks

partnered on our heater's cramp.
At the window, you breathe and spell
our names against the weather,

against the steel-shock of flakes on flesh,
strange tracks spiralling, widening and widening
while I draw down into my blankets.

The hushed circle of your lamp,
left on behind dark glass, just how things are wasted,
snow elsewhere, or desire.

FREYA AND OD

Waiting, I'm never where you're not,
sitting in the window square,

sun glinting off the snowbroth.
Why shouldn't this tinselled patch

be your side of the bed at dawn,
that tree root your foot,

seeking air from under-sheet?
It is nearly our hour

and we are plummeting towards spring.
You have pulled me into season,

the blossom bud-hearted,
earth wet-black with last year's leaves,

death, everywhere. A plane frets
the branches. Something is always

leaving, like your name,
falcon-feathered, rising in me by degrees.

BRISINGAMEN

When it rains, she leaves
her dress on the sand

while willows twin,
their echoes drifting

as she floats, her bare legs
bright below the undertow.

Comets in the shapes
of perch and minnow

prophesise much.
Miles into the dark,

you feel how her necklace
warms to your touch.

BOX OF SWANS

Maybe because it was quiet
one of those last nights
she gave me a box which couldn't be opened.

Red velvet, worn at the edges
and flocked with swans
oriental, blown ash and cinder,

necks curled like violins
down-tuned by the whicker of wings.
Something inside rang in her hand.

Afterwards, I forced the lock,
two silver balls nested,
and closed inside, a bell

chimed a memory which couldn't have been mine,
you picking me up in the back field,
from the plackets of hawthorn

wind feathering your hair across my cheek,
so that I could see the swans fly
singing from the weir towards the sea.

NAMING OF THE BIRDS

Only tinnitus, they said,
his ear nestled in the pillow.

Birds strung along his faulty nerve,
his telephone wire.

Cormorants on his black canal
clamoured from the water,

at the doves, their blood-murmur
singing through his branched veins.

In the shower, he trilled his fistful
of notes. But sunset brought quiet,

the wren-thin rib cages
of his children, rising, falling.

CHOOSING LAVENDER FOR YOUR FATHER'S GRAVE

Hardy, at least, lavender,
like the word for mist,
the sky's sullen freight.

Your cigarette-pull churned
in the wind against the stone,
your whole north burned.

Then let the road be silent,
hush the rooks at their coughing,
observe the still pines, your grief of flowers.

OH LIE DEAD

the amethyst, shoe polish,
terrible gold.

Light betrays an empty square
sparrows fray the remains
of morning, bold with quiet.

Somewhere, there is a room
filled almost entirely with hair.
Rain blurs letters

singing absolutely nothing,
shrives from the earth
a filling, a button.

MIND THE GAP

She sat
at Embankment
to hear his voice
telling passengers where to step,
above the tracks, the fusillade of sparks.

How many times
had stars come into eloquence
through their bedroom window?
That night she reached for a husband
seemingly just stepped out, but dead for years and years.

KVALØYSLETTA

Fish hung, salted in the eaves
like soles from the shoes
of the missing

sand dark with snow-melt
where the sea kissed
and searching kissed

and at the altar,
the one you lost long ago
about to leap to water,

before you kneel
and take to your lips
one pale shoulder

in tigered waves
decide if your own raftered chest
can survive what remains, what has changed.

SHARP VELVET

You had never tasted pomegranates,
so we huddled in our coats,
sat on our gloves
to keep them from the wind.

I taught you how to dig your thumbnails
and split the pith, peel back membrane
to show the clustered eyes.
You purled each scarlet seed
with a toothpick. Let one fall.

And when you murmured
in your sleep, vowels sprouting
from your stained mouth,
I thought of our tree,
nudging through earth-rind,
the morning's harvest of frost.

BYANNA'S SUNDAY

*The Sunday before Yule, boil a cow's head and keep the skull. Light a candle
in the eye socket.*

Dark heaves against the window,
and beyond that, the sea
murmuring pebbles to the line
of crusted weed, tumbling back.

Skim the fat from the pot,
in silvery spots, like coins
for drowned sailors. Plenty shrink
to the size of gulls, following

herring lanes, then sink or come
home again, but now, the cow's head
bobs, the meat floats free,
skull as bare as the rocks on the hill

which tomorrow will be tided
in Yule light. Ready then, the candles,
the tallow and wicks for the socket,
against the sun's last surge, gold beams
through our shallow, peopled water.

A YEAR WITHOUT WEATHER

Those first few days
we only noticed how the light had changed:

glass jigsawed on the floor,
drink all in fingers down the wall
and a sink's-worth of dirty dishes.
All things at the edge of rot, the bloom
we had not seen in the sun.

We stayed outside
while land lay flat as the tablecloth.
Fogged with mould, we found
sheep skulls to scent for rain,
recited the shepherd's charm
to the gone red sky. But here our tongues lit,
seeking a new forecast for weatherless.

BONE HARVEST

Stags slough their velvet
in bloody tatters. Each morning

I mark their prints in the mud
by the wrack, their rutting done,

and nine days left to hunt.
I promised my sword for this.

Above the fanged leaves in the furrow,
the sun passes over the bracken,

pesters the eyes of a bald buck,
pedicles bloodied. Somewhere, then,
I will find his antlers, my bone harvest.

THE SALMON

Because there's no such thing
as 'just one drink down The Salmon'
and because we took the shortcut back
through the manor house gardens,
where you hooked the barbed wire up
with three fingers, for me to duck,
still laughing from the graffiti
at the local Budgens, OUT to TROUT.
Because the last light at the lodge
was still on when we stopped in the silvered field –

Read this at 2 a.m. ,
when you're in the place you've found
instead of sleep, with the windows open
and a halo of snow around the stars,
until you arrive at the hollow of grass,
the night fine-tuning itself to absolute dark.
Then, having just missed me,
leave a different way,
and find yourself still plucking grass
from your clothes, days later.

GARDENS

There's something about
the peak of inebriation
when I'll see the golden bottle of whisky
tipped on its side
the cans indented by the ghost of your hand
or the way you examine
the still-lit tip of your cigarette
before you flick it away
but I still have to add the stars
or the floodlit shadows from next door's patio
those callow poetics
which leave me envious
of the empty glass by your elbow
that you're just about to knock over and smash.

BELA LUGOSI

We're allowed up late,
watching the screen between spread fingers.
Dracula taped off the TV. We clatter through ads.

Adult voices honk in the next room,
above the cello's swell, the painted backdrops:
mountains, castles, rural shrines.

One glimpse of blood would keep us hushed
for hours, kiting down lace wedding gowns
inked black as bats. Our faces clammy as theirs.

This is a good bit, every so often, someone's dad
says from the doorway, mouth stained with Shiraz.
The empty coffin's velvet should have been that red.

Still, all night, I hear the water pipes tapping
like he's coming back, shadowed black and white
intent on a Technicolor sunrise.

CUTTINGS

And one morning, you just wake up and like gardening.
Start to wonder if the soil is acid or alkali.
Name the one robin who follows your trowel as you hack the bad dirt
        the builders left behind:
smashed glass, rubble, old bathroom tiles –
you might have done something about it, before, but now it's the landlord's job,
and you won't lay a lawn for the next poor sod.
Grow seeds on the windowsill, water them from a tablespoon.
The camomile's going well, but the sage hasn't sprouted.
The acer she grew from a cutting at the old house is probably worth more
        than a month's rent now.
You picked up a price tag at the garden centre last week,
lured by the familiar curl of the mascara-brush leaves, and dropped it quickly.
The second year is different, everyone says, you can watch things coming back.
It seems things take time, good earth, and rain to put down roots
though seeds can spread, and pretty leaves
will turn from shade, seeking new sun
everywhere, even in your own garden.

MY GRANDMOTHER'S GRANDFATHER

I watched her dream back to Lerwick,
her chair hollowed to fit her,
printing withered lips on water glasses
the shade of the sand on Muckle Roe.
She dammed the North Sea there
with wet, gritted handfuls
and mouse-earred chickweed
shuddered white,
sky dark as an under-wing.

Down on the *aer*,
above the rush and *kurr* of the waves,
fish bellies bloomed under thin blades.
She told me everything she knew about salt,
how it split her mother's fingers,
waiting for her father to surface.

Land-locked, we watch at the window,
for the crooked flecks of gulls
fussing over scraps on deck
like bright drops shaken from an oar.
Through washing lines, roof tiles
his sea-voice floats, stiff with spindrift,
I'm still here, come find me.

SKADHI

Look to the hunter, above the dog,
those stars were his eyes.
Far above our mountains, earth roots firm
against the hurled questions of wolves.

Not long until frost will foam
our floors, a dowry.

Fair-footed one, we walk,
the world here halved
between sea and sky
as it thaws to morning.

I will navigate by those
two tossed cinders,
even here, where your pious waves
flay themselves, penitent.

CHRISTMAS EVE ON NORRIS RISE

That night the road slept.
Her room was sky-black
and it didn't take us long:
train tickets, old horoscopes,
a recipe she never tried,
folded, flashed bright jay-blue.

The magazine cover
a scribble-lark,
a shy yellowhammer snagged in the bush.
There's a trick to it,
she used to say,
fanning out wings and creasing tails.

My nested hands thatched on the sill,
blowing out doves like wounded stars
to ignite against the dark,
knowing the first drift of light
would ruin them.

In the morning,
let the neighbours wonder at the birds,
their silent, stubborn carols.

TWO FOR JOY

Below a dog tied to a pine snuffles in mulch –
this way, that way – sneezes.
Two walkers copulate, pink in the wind that parts the heather,
that stranger sea, so we're here,
golden in the shocking honey sun
the wind keeps blowing out. Faster than thought, that air is,
enough to whip back one bladed shoulder, purple moor screaming.
Old One Eye worries that we might not come back,
and like camera spool, memory might be soured by sunlight.
Who is to say what will stay? Years later, those walkers,
dog long gone and them to new love,
might scent through an office window
rain-dark pines and feel again those feathered needles,
something they thought they'd lost – had lost.

MERRIE DANCERS

— We called them the Merrie Dancers,
she said, the Northern Lights.

On the final day of the old year,
I was called home
to see my uncle leaning over,
telling her it was ok to leave,
her legs peeled to bone
beneath the hospital sheets.

So she clung to the arm that held her,
where the dark swells with ship's bells,
that old star-fox sparking the night
blush and green above the sea,

where the plunge will numb,
her feet striking three in a waltz,
past the tumble of cooper's barrels,
herring scales, the empty clam shells,
sipping their thirst at the surf's edge.

PUB LUNCH

At the end of your tether,
I hunch over *Rose and Crown* scampi,
bench wood warm under my palms.

On the river, a swan lumbers to air,
black webs tucked and curses
at a man chugging his boat around,

pale under a mildewed lifejacket.
A bee trickles on the lip
of your glass. You swat and miss,

sending it into shivering flight,
unseaming chubby jointed legs,
coarse yellow hairs. Unhook the sting

until all that are left are the quarks
which tumble like pollen grains.
You're not listening, you say.

STEALING FROM HER GARDEN

We were sent out here, as children
to rub the stone Buddha's belly for luck.
Tonight, there's just a spider uncurling,
all elbows down his laughing chest.
There's a light behind the new front door,
the smear of my face in the window,
a ghost in her house.

My uncle's drunk, swears there's no-one in,
digs through the pestering weeds
for something to plant under her oak
and over her ashes.

His shovel snicks the earth
around her fireweed
whittled to a winter stalk,
just two pink flowers tossed
like sparks above a bonfire.
The chalk roots are wrong,
bone in the smoke of moonlight.
I should've worn gloves,
he pinches the flesh of his hands,
as if to draw the whole of her dying
out like a splinter.

AMOK

Here, the fish is steamed
in a woven basket of leaves.
Candles crimson through paper,
belled into lanterns
strung stagewards.

Light blanks the hung sheet,
while behind it, the children
are blind, or deaf.

Drums. Figures flee from home.
Two monkeys fight to the death.
One buffalo, held too far off
fades into static. Strings whine.

Six thousand miles away,
in the kind of place
that still has last year's tinsel
caught in tape above the doorframe,
you sit and twist your wedding ring
like a dial, trying to bring something else
back into focus.

LOI KRATONG

Wrapped in silk, we walked to the moat.
Children surfaced like seals,
splashed after floats to sink them.

We lit candles on the water,
wicks almost too damp to catch.

I kept my wish on my tongue.

The next day, men with bamboo poles
and rolled-up sleeves
fished for remains,

petals, banana leaves, pins.
The river spirit, too, was quiet.

Whatever you wished for, say it again.

SPIRIT HOUSES

The dead return to us in dreams,
shunning golden spirit houses
on every corner, and the offerings:
incense, too-green Fanta,
Buddha's half-lid gaze.

Just like you,
being five months dead,
returning in the stammered ammo
of a bird, shadowing the plastic roof,
claws a promise of rain.

Often speaking, as a girl in Shetland,
of the German pilot swooping low,
his ghost-cross bent across
grass and rock, the shagged coast,
and him being close enough
that seventy years later
you could still describe your running,
and his red hair.

SOM TAM

Soi dogs scrounged under tables
for scraps, savvy past sandalled feet,
                                     red silk

the sudden   slate-slab side of an elephant,
round eye rolling for sugarcane, pomelo.

We shared a beer with ice,
sweating more than the bottle

grinding chillies, garlic, shining limes,

whole crabs frilled blue,
                        mushrooms I thought were seaweed.

Years later, in this kitchen,
I halve and crush chillies,
                        seeds clinging to the blade.

When I touch my eyes,
the sting is the very luxury of avoiding you,

now that you're here no longer.

INSIDE THE BELLY OF AN OX

No labour to slip inside,
one foot braced
on the row of teeth
like broken stones,
the massive tongue.
A lung's worth to slide
down the gullet to the belly.
So dark, you must imagine
hooves sparking against flint,
sun on curved spine,
your tail losing against spiralling flies.

You might expect two eye-holes
to let light in, like a child's Halloween mask,
but you are far too deep for that.
Just the wet flex of muscle,
sweating against cart rope
as if you haul the whole earth
underfoot, two thousand temples,
as old as the grass, the dust,
the bone of your horn, found lying
in ochre and carved by the hunter.
Even as Orion rises above parched trees,
you pause and remember,
the spilled blood, the rough blushed walls.

SLEIGHT OF HAND

Severed, that fourth finger
by tiger-tooth or bicycle chain.
He told the tale differently every time.

Goaded, he'd rummage his pocket
past tobacco tin, his pin-up lighter,
and flourish-thumb his digit back to socket –

and then gone again. Death left
no finger, but still I thought of that trick,
and how I might still find it, years later,

curled and parched in a box of his things,
coal and silver mooning his nail,
the way the War had brought him back, but wrong.

Then I might palm the bone,
the foxed flesh with sleight of hand
and know that I too have something to hide.

LINDISFARNE

A fish, stranded like a flag,
eye already gone.

You tapped my shoulder
to turn our backs on
the still-standing arch.

Our bare feet sinking,
we followed the sea road
towards distant seagrass, pilgrim seals,

a man at prayer to his sunken rear axle,
crouched claggy-kneed in the sand.

SILVER BIRCH

His hair hanging
in my face
will someday be silver.

Feel the knotholes
in his spine,
skin peeled
and bright in the bedroom,
ripples of bark
which we will count
to lull his ringed heart to sleep.

Shame,
his breath
was just the drifting catkins,
dawn-pale as the east. Or the axe blade.

BRESSAY COO

Divorce is a passport
that sent us all different ways.

Homesickness for steps hollowed
under years and years of feet,

the slow fame all summer
of being *Lizzie's bairns from London*

unlocks this lighthouse,
sun simmering across the North Sea,

one finger-touch enough to spin
the whole lens, suspended in mercury

that might flash danger, or a return
to sailors in the dark, the spindrift mist,

a sunstone you remembered
many years later, when you left home

squinting against the anchorless dusk,
the last of your old life boxed up,
the many rocks to wreck upon.

MISTLETOE

A real malarkey of magpies scatter as we pass, coughing
racket. December, and a whole day of dusk, headlights
winking through thin trees. We've stopped for a bet —
you say rookeries, I, mistletoe. And though I've never
seen it before, I am sure that the tangles blousing high
branches aren't merely nests. We shine your phone, I am
right. I plant one hand on your chest for the kiss, know-
ing that one day, this hand might run through ash, or
else, yours through mine. Whether it is better to leave,
or be the one left, remains to be seen.

THE WRECK

That last day
we found the wreck ourselves,
past the old white lighthouse
and bitter scrub grass.

Jackets over arms
swung like deadweights,
trouser cuffs dark, salt-heavy.
We stamped off sand up Seagate Road.

You brought it home
in the flooded dark,
dredging up the hull of my hand.
All night, the sea was a word you couldn't catch.

BRAGI AS A GOLDFINCH

singing in the apple-blossom

split yolk wing with a vein
of blood through the face

I never used to understand Spring

a charm of goldfinches
blushing among the early buds

a kingfisher, a bright needle
stitching the trees to the bank
the bank to the river

I never used to understand Spring
but in the late sun,
see how there is a time
for all that has worn through
to be mended

you say that you can already see Autumn
the lick of red in the goldfinch
boasting in the early buds
spilt egg below the nest

SUNDAY MORNING ATTICS

Your chest like some sort of tyrant attic,
needing endless Sundays
to sift the archaeology there.

We are so rarely first
or second, or even third
to hear the words that let you in

past all the childhood clutter
the old cot, broken train
the photographs of others, some dead,

and to sift through sinew,
past bone, dare say – love – like that
could only disturb the others there.

I know too. This is not
the first morning I've lain
almost blissed to watch the pigeons

rumbling in the early sun.
We find familiar positions
to rest a hand, hook a foot.

Soon, though, one of us must rise,
perhaps open the window. A gap,
to let in whatever is coming next.

YEARS WITHOUT WEATHER

After years without weather
the eldest among us spoke of snow.

I struggled to remember:
the cold-white of feather, or bone,

the brackish churn at the roadside
by dawn, after last night's drift.

You said the Northmen had a hundred words,
or more, for snow

and I wracked my tongue
for birch trees, those first game tracks

spelling an age of black bark
in crusted ice.
The silence before the first fall.

LOKI

Drops tumble from rock,
scatter ripples like minnows.

This used to be torture,
but now I count the rings,

a tree-age held in tremulous silver,
too soon flared to the edge

of the pool, and gone.
The serpent too, coils.

Even with eyes shut, you can tell
whether the moon or sun circles,

veins pink, or else lids ghosted,
like the voice of my son

thrumming through these chains.
Only when she takes the bowl

from my face does the pain come
and I shudder. In the distance,
I see a ship, all, all of them dead.

FIMBULWINTER

Just how I imagined the house as a child,
locked empty in the day
without us to map it —

I've found it. Now I push through forks,
forested and coaxing kitchen shadows
while spoons bloom like magnolias.

I feel my way upstairs,
the pine boards split
to count an age. One hundred, two.

Vines cling to the posts,
and from somewhere, a river laps
slithering bright as lightning,

floor rubbed raw to granite.
Here, the day is dim,
dusk silting low through the hallway.

The carpet is frozen into hackles,
like the nape of the wolf I half-see
sloping into the bedroom,

lips snarled into the beginnings of words,
and my breath comes cold.
Underfoot, bones of small animals snap,

then larger: a piano-keyed jawbone,
femur. Beyond where the curtains
should hang, a stag cocks one ear,

hounding, at his hooves,
a tattered crow, blood-shocked
with both wings broken.

I still remember the duvet,
laced with hoarfrost,
the winter-lake crack as I pulled it back.

Too bad, then, that everything we dream,
we dream in the dark.
I lie down, touch your arm.

BIRTHDAY CANDLES

Budded flame,
fish-quick
that deep glint in the dark.

Gathered around your table
we ask you to make a wish
pickled in candle brine-light.

We bloom like squids,
singing pale at your portside
until you quiet the wick.

Imagine, in the grey smoke-stain they leave,
a grey herring-light breaking
over the black North sea, your burning longboat.

NOTES

Gullveig – Gullveig was a powerful Volva (wise or cunning woman) who was speared and burnt three times by the Aesir. Each time she was reborn.

Yggdrasil – Odin hung on the world tree, Yggdrasil, for nine nights, seeking knowledge. In the 'Havamal', it says that he 'sacrificed himself to himself', piercing himself with a spear. At the end of the nine days, he seized the runes.

Volva – Odin raises a dead wise-woman, or Volva, in order to learn about the fate of his son Baldr. She confirms that both Baldr and his wife Nana will be feasting in Helheim, the land of the dead, soon.

Baldr – In an attempt to counter the Volva's prediction, Baldr's mother Frigga makes everything in the Nine Worlds swear an oath not to harm him. She only missed the mistletoe, growing just outside of Asgard, as she thought it was too small to harm him.

Frigg – Frigg didn't ask the mistletoe, believing it too small to hurt Baldr. Loki discovered this, and when the Gods were playing by casting weapons at the unharmed Baldr, he gave a shaft of mistletoe to the blind God Hod, Baldr's brother. Hod shot Baldr, who died.

When They Ask What I Told You – Odin, in disguise as Gagnrath ('the gain-counsellor') journeyed to the home of Vafthruthnir in order to see who possessed the most wisdom. They answered each other's questions, until Gagnrath asked what Odin whispered into the ear of his son Baldr when he lay on the pyre. Vafthruthnir realised that his visitor could only be Odin, as only Odin would possess that knowledge. ,

Helroad – After Baldr's death, Hermod 'The Swift' borrowed Odin's horse Sleipnir and journeyed down to Helheim, in order to ask Hel, the Goddess of Death, to release Baldr and return him to life.

Lunula – A lunula is a crescent-moon shaped amulet, given for protection.

Freya and Od – Freya's husband Od is away wandering, and she mourns his absence by crying golden tears. She possesses a cloak of falcon feathers, which allows her to transform into a falcon.

Brisingamen – Brisingamen is the name of the goddess Freya's necklace. Four dwarfs crafted it. When Freya saw it, she desired it so much that she offered them gold and silver for it. They refused, instead promising that she could have the necklace if she spent one night with each of them. She did this and claimed the necklace.

Bone Harvest – The God Freyr falls in love with a giantess, Gerðr. He gives his servant his sword, in return for him bringing Gerðr back to be his wife. She consents, but says that she will first wait nine nights, leaving Freyr pining. Later, at Ragnarök, he is forced to fight Surtr with an antler, having given up his sword.

Skadhi – Following the murder of her father, *Þjazi*, Skadhi marched to Asgard to demand revenge. Odin cast her father's eyes up into the sky to become stars, Loki made her laugh by tying his genitals to a goat, and Odin promised that she could have any husband from among them, providing that she chose by only looking at their feet. She chose Njord.

Two for Joy – Odin has two ravens, Hugin and Munin, who fly out over the worlds every day and bring back news to him. Their names mean 'thought' and 'memory.'

Bragi – Bragi is the Norse god of poetry. He is married to Idunna, the goddess who tends the apples that renew the lives of the gods.

Loki – Following Baldr's death, Loki breaks frith with the gods, and so they transform his sons into wolves and bind him to a rock in a cave with their intestines. Skadhi fixes a serpent above him, which drips poison down on his face. Loki's wife, Sigyn, waits with him, catching the poison in a bowl. When she has to empty the bowl, the poison drips onto Loki's face and he shakes in pain, causing earthquakes. At Ragnarök, Loki will free himself and wage war on all the worlds, journeying in his ship Naglfar, made entirely from the nails of the dead.

Fimbulwinter – Fimbulwinter is the final, three-year-long winter which signals the coming of Ragnarök.

ACKNOWLEDGEMENTS

Some of these poems have been previously published in
*Amok, Brittle Star, The Ekphrastic Review, The Lighthouse
Journal, Someone Else's Photograph*, and *Stand Magazine*.
'Longship' was highly commended in *The Interpreter's
House* Open Competition.

With thanks to my editor, Dr Alex Wylie, for his help
and insight, and also to Edwin Smet for his wonderful
cover design. Thanks also to Dr Todd Swift and Eyewear
Publishing for their wise guidance and encouragement.
Finallly, thanks to the judge of the Melita Hume Prize,
Colette Sensier, for her kind feedback.